GAYLORD

How to Analyze the Works of

F. SCOTT FITZGERALD

by Maggie Combs

ABDO
Publishing Company

Essential Critiques

How to Analyze the Works of

F. SCOTT FITZGERALD

by Maggie Combs

Content Consultant: Joe Hughes
Department of English Literature, University of Minnesota

Credits

Published by ABDO Publishing Company, 8000 West 78th Street, Edina, Minnesota 55439. Copyright © 2012 by Abdo Consulting Group, Inc. International copyrights reserved in all countries. No part of this book may be reproduced in any form without written permission from the publisher. The Essential Library™ is a trademark and logo of ABDO Publishing Company.

Printed in the United States of America,
North Mankato, Minnesota
062011
092011

 THIS BOOK CONTAINS AT LEAST 10% RECYCLED MATERIALS.

Editor: Amy Van Zee
Copy Editor: Sarah Beckman
Interior Design and Production: Kazuko Collins
Cover Design: Marie Tupy

Library of Congress Cataloging-in-Publication Data
Combs, Maggie, 1985-
  How to analyze the works of F. Scott Fitzgerald / by Maggie Combs.
    p. cm. -- (Essential critiques)
  Includes bibliographical references and index.
  ISBN 978-1-61783-092-1
  1. Fitzgerald, F. Scott (Francis Scott), 1896-1940--Criticism and interpretation-- Juvenile literature. I. Title.

  PS3511.I9Z578 2011
  813'.52--dc22

                              2011006302

Table of Contents

Chapter

1

Introduction to Critiques

What Is Critical Theory?

What do you usually do when you read a book?
You probably absorb the specific language style of
the book. You learn about the characters as they are
developed through thoughts, dialogue, and other
interactions. You may like or dislike a character
more than others. You might be drawn in by the plot
of the book, eager to find out what happens at the
end. Yet these are only a few of many possible ways
of understanding and appreciating a book. What
if you are interested in delving more deeply? You
might want to learn more about the author and how
his or her personal background is reflected in the
book. Or you might want to examine what the book
says about society—how it depicts the roles of

women and minorities, for example. If so, you have entered the realm of critical theory.

Critical theory helps you learn how various works of art, literature, music, theater, film, and other endeavors either support or challenge the way society behaves. Critical theory is the evaluation and interpretation of a work using different philosophies, or schools of thought. Critical theory can be used to understand all types of cultural productions.

There are many different critical theories. If you are analyzing literature, each theory asks you to look at the work from a different perspective. Some theories address social issues, while others focus on the writer's life or the time period in which the book was written or set. For example, the critical theory that asks how an author's life affected the work is called biographical criticism. Other common schools of criticism include historical criticism, feminist criticism, psychological criticism, and New Criticism, which examines a work solely within the context of the work itself.

What Is the Purpose of Critical Theory?

Critical theory can open your mind to new ways of thinking. It can help you evaluate a book from a new perspective, directing your attention to issues and messages you may not otherwise recognize in a work. For example, applying feminist criticism to a book may make you aware of female stereotypes perpetuated in the work. Applying a critical theory to a book helps you learn about the person who created it or the society that enjoyed it. You can also explore how the work is perceived by current cultures.

How Do You Apply Critical Theory?

You conduct a critique when you use a critical theory to examine and question a work. The theory you choose is a lens through which you can view the work, or a springboard for asking questions about the work. Applying a critical theory helps you think critically about the work. You are free to question the work and make an assertion about it. If you choose to examine a book using biographical theory, for example, you want to know how the author's personal background or education inspired or shaped the work. You could explore why the author was drawn to the story. For instance, are there any parallels between a particular character's life and the author's life?

Forming a Thesis

Ask your question and find answers in the work or other related materials. Then you can create a thesis. The thesis is the key point in your critique. It is your argument about the work based on the tenets, or beliefs, of the theory you are using. For example, if you are using biographical theory to ask how the author's life inspired the work, your thesis could be worded as follows: Writer Teng Xiong, raised in refugee camps in

> ### How to Make a Thesis Statement
>
> In a critique, a thesis statement typically appears at the end of the introductory paragraph. It is usually only one sentence long and states the author's main idea.

Southeast Asia, drew upon her experiences to write the novel *No Home for Me*.

Providing Evidence

Once you have formed a thesis, you must provide evidence to support it. Evidence might take the form of examples and quotations from the work itself—such as dialogue from a character. Articles about the book or personal interviews with the author might also support your ideas. You may wish to address what other critics have written about the work. Quotes from these individuals may help support your claim. If you find any quotes or examples that contradict your thesis, you will need to create an argument against them. For instance: Many critics have pointed to the protagonist of *No Home for Me* as a powerless victim of circumstances. However, in the chapter "My Destiny," she is clearly depicted as someone who seeks to shape her own future.

How to Support
a Thesis Statement

A critique should include several arguments. Arguments support a thesis claim. An argument is one or two sentences long and is supported by evidence from the work being discussed.

Organize the arguments into paragraphs. These paragraphs make up the body of the critique.

In This Book

In this book, you will read summaries of famous novels and short stories by writer F. Scott Fitzgerald, each followed by a critique. Each critique will use one theory and apply it to one work. Critical thinking sections will give you a chance to consider other theses and questions about the work. Did you agree with the author's application of the theory? What other questions are raised by the thesis and its arguments? You can also find out what other critics think about each particular book. Then, in the You Critique It section in the final pages of this book, you will have an opportunity to create your own critique.

Look for the Guides

Throughout the chapters that analyze the works, thesis statements have been highlighted. The box next to the thesis helps explain what questions are being raised about the work. Supporting arguments have been underlined. The boxes next to the arguments help explain how these points support the thesis. Look for these guides throughout each critique.

Author F. Scott Fitzgerald

2

A Closer Look at F. Scott Fitzgerald

F. Scott Fitzgerald mastered the art of the coming-of-age story in a historical period during which the United States was going through its own adolescence. His most respected and famous work, *The Great Gatsby*, is one of the great American novels and one of the most taught novels in the United States. From his quiet childhood in St. Paul, Minnesota, to the flashy French Riviera, Fitzgerald and his wife, Zelda, eventually became two of the most prominent icons of America's Jazz Age.

Disconnected Youth

Francis Scott Key Fitzgerald was born in St. Paul on September 24, 1896, to Edward Fitzgerald and Mary McQuillan Fitzgerald (called Mollie). Francis Scott was named after his distant relative,

Francis Scott Key, who authored the lyrics to the "Star-Spangled Banner." Francis Scott's father was from Maryland, and his mother came from a wealthy Irish Catholic family in St. Paul. Mollie Fitzgerald spoiled Francis Scott. Because his father was unable to keep a job, the young boy grew up in an unsettled home. The family lived in various places in New York before eventually moving back to St. Paul and living with financial help from Mollie's wealthy family. Francis Scott did not do well in school, but he was an excellent storyteller from an early age. His dreams of success would be achieved through his tenacious spirit.

Francis Scott believed that attending an East Coast school would be essential to his future greatness. So when he failed the entrance exams for Princeton, he used his power of language to convince the Princeton selection committee that he was an extraordinary candidate. Although he would attend Princeton from 1913 to 1917 without graduating, Francis Scott took great pride in the prestige of his college for the rest of his life. Instead of finishing college, he enlisted in the US Army in 1917. But World War I (1914–1918) ended shortly thereafter, and he never saw combat.

Love and Zelda

In 1918, Fitzgerald was stationed in
Montgomery, Alabama, where he met Zelda Sayre.
Zelda was the kind of woman he always wrote
about: young, beautiful, wealthy, loved by others,
and somewhat wild. Fitzgerald was one of many
suitors, but their relationship soon became serious.
Fitzgerald proposed many times to Zelda, but

F. Scott and
Zelda Fitzgerald
spent the first
years of their
marriage in New
York City. They
traveled often
during their
marriage and
lived in Europe.

she refused to marry him until he was financially secure. In 1919, Fitzgerald traveled to New York City to work on publishing his first novel, which would help him win Zelda's heart.

Finally in 1920, when Zelda began to consider other men, Fitzgerald's novel *This Side of Paradise* was published to outstanding reviews. Fitzgerald married Zelda immediately and brought her to live with him in New York City. Together in New York, Fitzgerald and Zelda began to live the wild and wealthy lifestyle of his dreams. *Flappers and Philosophers*, Fitzgerald's first short story collection, was published in 1920. *Flapper* is a term used to describe the unconventional modern women of the post-World War I era.

Zelda gave birth to a baby girl, Francis Scott "Scottie" Fitzgerald, in 1921. Scottie was to be the Fitzgeralds' only child, and she was raised mostly by her nanny. Fitzgerald's second novel, *The Beautiful and Damned*, was published in 1922 as well as another short story collection titled *Tales of the Jazz Age*. As Fitzgerald and Zelda engaged continually in their frantic flapper lifestyle, their lives became increasingly chaotic. Their partying and drinking were causing problems.

The Expatriate Years

In 1924, the chaos became too much, so the Fitzgeralds sailed to Europe and spent the winter in Rome. Although they changed cities and social groups, their lives continued to lack healthy structure and work. They spent most of the next two years in France, their time divided between Paris and the French Riviera. The Fitzgeralds surrounded themselves with Americans living abroad. In Paris, Fitzgerald met American writer Ernest Hemingway, and despite Zelda's dislike of Hemingway, he and Fitzgerald became close friends.

Fitzgerald's friendship with Hemingway was only the beginning of the problems in the Fitzgeralds' marriage. While on the French Riviera, Zelda had an affair with a French aviator. The affair quickly ended, but it was only a small part of Zelda's downward spiral. During their time in Europe, Zelda grew more restless and desperate for her own fame and success. Zelda frightened their acquaintances with her unusual behavior.

A Slow Death

In 1925, Fitzgerald published *The Great Gatsby*. In 1926, *All the Sad Young Men*, Fitzgerald's third short story collection, was published. Although it was not immediately respected, *The Great Gatsby* marks the pinnacle of Fitzgerald's career. In terms of recognition, nothing he wrote afterward would ever top this masterpiece. Despite its place in the American literary canon, the novel marked the beginning of the slow death of Fitzgerald's career and marriage.

Soon after *The Great Gatsby* was published, Zelda's mental health began to rapidly deteriorate. She was eventually diagnosed with schizophrenia and institutionalized, first in Switzerland and later in Baltimore, Maryland. As her mental health crumbled, Fitzgerald fell deeper into the pit of alcoholism that he would not acknowledge. During the 1930s, as Zelda was in and out of hospitals, Fitzgerald often lived in nearby hotels.

The stress of Zelda's mental illness and Fitzgerald's increasing dependence on alcohol made it difficult for him to concentrate on his work. It was eight years before Fitzgerald published another novel, *Tender Is the Night*, in 1934. This novel is darker than his others, focusing on a mentally ill woman and her physician husband. The heaviness of the novel is a window into Fitzgerald's own

feelings as he dealt with Zelda's illness and the shock of the Great Depression.

Fitzgerald wrote short stories to keep the family financially afloat during this difficult period, but he found short story writing tedious. In 1935, he published his final short story collection, *Taps at Reveille*. He also tried his hand at screenwriting in Hollywood, but he was not successful. Fitzgerald continued in Hollywood, working on his next novel, *The Last Tycoon*. But he would not finish the book. On December 21, 1940, Fitzgerald had a heart attack that took his life. He was buried in Rockville, Maryland.

On the whole, Fitzgerald experienced moderate success during his lifetime. After his death, however, his critical praise increased.

A statue of Fitzgerald sits in St. Paul, Minnesota. Fitzgerald was born in the state, and Minnesota is the setting for much of "Winter Dreams."

3

An Overview of "Winter Dreams"

"Winter Dreams" is best known as the story that
Fitzgerald used to experiment with the themes
and characters he would later write into *The Great
Gatsby*. "Winter Dreams" was first published in
1922 in *Metropolitan Magazine* and later published
in 1926 in a collection of short stories titled *All the
Sad Young Men*.

Dreams Born

"Winter Dreams" begins in the summer. Dexter
Green is a caddy at an elite golf course in Black
Bear, Minnesota. However, Dexter is not a caddy
because his family needs the money—Dexter's
father owns a grocery store. Instead, Dexter caddies
to make extra pocket money. He is happy as a caddy
until he encounters young Judy Jones. She is the

daughter of Mr. Mortimer Jones, a man who Dexter has idealized as the kind of upper-class businessman he would like to become. Judy makes Dexter feel the social inferiority of being a caddy. Dexter quits his job immediately after meeting Judy with dreams of becoming the kind of upper-class man who Judy would notice.

Dreams Built

Dexter attends college on the East Coast and returns to Minnesota to open a laundry business. Through his use of special washing methods, he earns the loyalty of the upper class, and his laundry business becomes very successful. He makes enough money to climb to the upper-middle class, but the heights of the upper class still elude him. Dexter knows that no matter how much money he has, he will still be an outsider because his family has not been wealthy for generations before him. The upper class that he wants to join consists of old-money elite. *Old money* is a term for wealthy people whose families have been rich for several generations. No matter how much money Dexter makes, he cannot join their ranks unless he joins one of their families.

Dexter meets Judy at the golf course where he works and she plays.

Dexter comes a little closer to his dream when one of his old-money clients gives him a day pass to the golf course where he caddied as a teenager. While Dexter is golfing, he meets Judy again. She has developed into the most popular and beautiful woman Dexter has ever known. He is immediately attracted to her, and through a chance encounter with her on the lake, he becomes one of her many suitors. Although Dexter immediately falls in love with Judy, she returns his affections only some of the time—she appears to be in love with him one day and forgets about him the next. After a summer of longing after Judy, Dexter finally realizes that she will never marry him. He gives up on her just as she leaves to spend the winter in Florida.

While Judy is gone for the winter, Dexter becomes engaged to a sweet girl named Irene. They plan to marry the following September. But when Judy returns in May, Dexter's dreams overtake him. Judy seeks out Dexter and tells him that she wants to marry him. Dexter breaks off his engagement with Irene but finds himself competing with other suitors for Judy's attention, just as he had competed before. Judy's interest in Dexter lasts only for a month, and he ends up leaving the Midwest and training to fight in World War I.

Death of Dreams

The final chapter of this short story happens seven years later. Dexter is now living in New York. He meets a businessman from Detroit who mentions in passing that his friend married Judy. Dexter is outraged when the businessman describes Judy as pretty rather than beautiful. Dexter is also surprised to hear that the man she married does not treat her well and that her beauty has faded. He is shocked and appalled.

Dexter finally admits to himself that the dream is gone. After the businessman leaves, Dexter finds himself crying. He does not cry for Judy; he cries for himself. Judy was his dream—his ticket into the upper class—and now she has faded away. Dexter concludes that he cannot cry or care anymore, because the dream inside him has faded too.

Karl Marx was born in 1818 in what is now Germany.
He died in 1883.

How to Apply Marxist Criticism to "Winter Dreams"

No.2

What Is Marxist Criticism?

Marxist criticism is often mistakenly associated with the Communist Party, but it is not a political system. Instead, it is German philosopher and economist Karl Marx's complex theory of how nineteenth-century capitalism worked. Under capitalism, the economy is controlled by private individuals and groups instead of the government. The most basic claim of Marxism is that "getting and keeping economic power is the motive behind all social and political activities."[1] This struggle for money and power splits society into two major socioeconomic classes: those who have money and those who do not. The Marxist terms for these classes are the *bourgeoisie*, who control society and its wealth, and the *proletariat*, who perform manual labor and live in poverty. A Marxist understanding of literature includes digging into the economic motives behind the characters in the novel and sometimes the motive of the author.

In the United States, the class system is referred to primarily as lower class, middle class, and upper class. If the upper class is oppressing the middle class, there are ways in which the middle class is also oppressing the lower class. As is common in cases of oppression, the people who are being oppressed are, in turn, oppressing others with a lower socioeconomic condition.

But why do people stay oppressed? What stops them from rising up against their oppressors? One reason is that there is a complex system of beliefs and values that distracts people from their own oppression. Marx called this system of beliefs ideology. One such belief is that of the American dream. The American dream is the idea that all people, regardless of their socioeconomic background, can better their lives and move up among the classes through hard work and individualism. Marxists believe that the upper class uses this concept to keep the lower classes from revolting against their rule. When the lower classes believe that they can achieve the economic prosperity and power of the upper class, they do not want to rise against the upper class—they want to join it.

Marxist criticism is a lens through which to understand a piece of literature. A few questions will help readers find the ways a piece of literature represents the socioeconomic struggle. Marxist critics might ask: Does the story perpetuate capitalist ideals, such as the private ownership of property and the importance of a free market economy? On the opposite side, does the work critique capitalist values and the oppression of socioeconomic classes? Does the story support capitalism in some ways and Marxism in others? Does the story reflect the socioeconomic conditions of the time period in which it takes place?

Applying Marxist Criticism to "Winter Dreams"

On the surface, "Winter Dreams" is about adolescent hope and the disappointment of lost love. But what is happening beneath the surface? Focusing on Dexter's struggle with his middle-class background reveals a different kind of story—one with Marxist underpinnings, including the idea that the American dream is a veneer that keeps people from seeing the reality of social classes. Dexter dreams of becoming a member of the upper class, and Judy Jones symbolizes his dreams of becoming part of the social elite. Dexter is willing to give up everything to marry her. Dexter eventually gives up on the idea of marrying Judy, but he does not recognize the death of his dream until he hears that Judy's beauty has faded, and she has become just an average woman. Through the loss of his love for Judy, Dexter experiences the death of the American dream. This death reveals the deceptive nature of the American dream and symbolically frees Dexter from the confines of the American class system.

Dexter is born into a financially secure middle-class family, but their prosperity is not enough for Dexter.

Thesis Statement

The thesis statement reads: "Through the loss of his love for Judy, Dexter experiences the death of the American dream. This death reveals the deceptive nature of the American dream and symbolically frees Dexter from the confines of the American class system." The thesis addresses Marxist concepts of class systems and the ideology of the American dream.

Argument One

The author is now arguing her thesis statement. The first argument states: "Dexter is born into a financially secure middle-class family, but their prosperity is not enough for Dexter." This first argument sets the stage for the arguments to follow. Without this argument, the others would not make sense.

He believes the ideology of the American dream. He longs for something more, which he believes he can find in the upper class: old-money patrons of the golf course where Dexter works as a caddy. Dexter's American dream leads him to seek the approval of the upper class in a desperate attempt to become one of them. This is evidenced when he quits his job as a caddy. By believing the American dream, Dexter is not concerned about the potential oppression he experiences from the class above him because he is instead attempting to join that class. The American dream is a common theme among Fitzgerald's stories, and "Winter Dreams" is no exception. Fitzgerald called "Winter Dreams" his "[first] draft" of what would be his greatest story about the American dream, *The Great Gatsby*.[2]

Through Dexter's job as a caddy, he meets a young girl named Judy. Judy is symbolic of his dreams to become part of the upper class. Judy is the daughter of Mr. Mortimer Jones, a wealthy businessman who is the foremost character in Dexter's

Argument Two

The second argument states: "Judy is symbolic of his dreams to become part of the upper class." The main point of a paragraph should appear at the beginning of the paragraph, but it is not always the first sentence. This argument is also laying the groundwork for the arguments that follow.

dreams before he meets Judy. Dexter believed that if Mr. Jones was "among those who watched him in open-mouthed wonder," Dexter would be a proven member of the upper class.[3] As a caddy, admiration from Mr. Jones is only a desire, not a reality. Marrying Judy is Dexter's ticket to making his dream into a reality.

Fitzgerald describes Judy in language that marks her beauty and charm. If Judy is symbolic of the American dream, then the descriptions of her also describe the allure of the American dream. The reader feels the same desire for Judy that Dexter feels for her and for his dream of achieving upper-class status through marrying her. When Judy is young and Dexter's dream is just beginning, she is said to be "destined after a few years to be inexpressibly lovely and bring no end of misery to a great number of men."[4] After a few years pass and Dexter's dreams have become his purpose in life, he meets Judy again. She is now "arrestingly

Argument Three

Argument three states: "Fitzgerald describes Judy in language that marks her beauty and charm. If Judy is symbolic of the American dream, then the descriptions of her also describe the allure of the American dream." The author is again connecting Judy with the American dream. By describing Judy as desirable and alluring, the author argues that these descriptions apply to the American dream too.

beautiful," and the men with Dexter confess their attraction to her.[5] When Dexter kisses Judy, it is described as charity. Dexter is the middle-class boy who, without Judy's charity, will never make it into the society of the upper-class elite. Dexter becomes grateful for this inclusion, and his feelings of admiration for the upper class grow stronger. The allure of Judy is the allure of the American dream.

Because Judy is Dexter's only way to become a member of the upper class, he is willing to sacrifice everything else to have her. This further characterizes the attraction of the American dream. As a boy, Dexter gives up his successful job as a caddy and his

> **Argument Four**
> The fourth argument is: "Because Judy is Dexter's way to become a member of the upper class, he is willing to sacrifice everything else to have her. This further characterizes the attraction of the American dream." This argument shows the extent of Dexter's commitment to the American dream because of its exceeding allure.

ability to make money because Judy views him as inferior. Although Judy's low opinion of Dexter is based on his socioeconomic position, Dexter is still attracted to her. It is this first encounter with Judy that solidifies to Dexter that middle-class wealth is not enough for him. He must attain the heights of the upper class. As an adult, Dexter gives up his engagement to another girl to become one of Judy's many suitors. His fiancée is a nice girl, but Dexter knows that she cannot help him live the fantastic life of the upper class. His fiancée cannot compare to the dream of Judy, so when Judy comes to him asking him to marry her, he dumps his fiancée without regret. Even after Judy's passion for Dexter dies again, he does not regret that he forsook all to pursue his dream.

Argument Five

Argument five states: "Seven years later, Dexter hears that Judy has become a shadow of her previous self. Dexter finally recognizes that his American dream has died as well, and his eyes are opened to the lie he had believed for so long." This argument is the final step in proving the thesis.

Seven years later, Dexter hears that Judy has become a shadow of her previous self. Dexter finally recognizes that his American dream has died as well, and his eyes are opened to the lie he had believed for so long. In the final chapter of "Winter Dreams," Dexter hears of Judy through a friend. In the years since Dexter has seen her, the perception of Judy has changed dramatically. She is now described as only a "pretty girl" and a "nice girl."[6] Dexter gets very upset that her exquisite beauty no longer exists in the world, and he begins to cry. The tears are not for Judy, but for the loss of

his dream. He is upset that the only beauty left in the world is "the gray beauty of steel that withstands all time."[7] This description of steel demonstrates

A 1950 cover for *All the Sad Young Men*, the short story collection that contains "Winter Dreams"

that Dexter's dream of becoming part of the rarely working upper class rather than the laboring middle class has died. He even recognizes that his previous life at the golf course was "the country of illusion," which symbolizes the opening of his eyes to the illusion of the American dream.[8] In the final sentence of the story, Dexter recognizes that his American dream "will come back no more."[9]

Dexter's American dream is never realized—he never reaches the upper class. "Winter Dreams" demonstrates how the Marxist ideology of the American dream keeps the lower classes in their places. Instead of resenting the upper class for their elitism, Dexter is consumed by his belief that he can become one of them. The story ultimately shows the American dream to be a great deception.

Conclusion

The last paragraph summarizes all of the arguments and restates the thesis. This conclusion reiterates the Marxist idea that ideologies, such as the American dream, keep the lower classes from rebelling against the upper class.

Thinking Critically about "Winter Dreams"

Now it is your turn to assess the critique. Consider these questions:

1. The thesis statement asserts that the American dream is dead for Dexter. Do you agree? Explain.

2. Do the arguments support the thesis? Are there any arguments that could be changed or left out? If you were to add an argument to this essay, what would it be?

3. Conclusions are meant to summarize the essay, but they sometimes add a final thought to the essay as well. What does this conclusion say about the nature of the American dream? Do you agree with it? Why or why not?

Other Approaches

Analyzing the death of the American dream is only one way to apply Marxist criticism to "Winter Dreams." Look back at the questions that Marxists ask, and think about how you can apply one of those questions to create an entirely different approach to "Winter Dreams."

Classism Critique

While this essay focuses on Dexter's struggle to move from the middle class to the upper class, another effective essay could argue that because "Winter Dreams" focuses only on the two upper classes and ignores the poor, it is perpetuating the capitalist viewpoint that poor people are not worth writing about. This approach is using the idea of classism, where the value of a human being is based on the social class into which a human is born.

A thesis for this essay might state: By ignoring the poor people present in the background of the story, "Winter Dreams" reinforces the capitalist agenda that people born without money are not worth trying to understand. One of the arguments for this critique could mention that Fitzgerald's main character is a caddy who does not need to make money rather than one of the caddies who is working to survive.

Goods and Services

Karl Marx believed that communism would eventually replace capitalism. Under capitalism, Marx noted a discrepancy between workers and those who enjoyed the fruits of that work. The upper classes would always work less but enjoy a disproportionate amount of the goods and services produced by the poor, who do not have time or money to enjoy the goods and services they produce. Another approach to "Winter Dreams" could investigate this discrepancy.

A thesis for such an essay could state: "Winter Dreams" highlights Marx's criticism of capitalism—that the working class will never be free from work because they will always be needed to produce goods and services for the upper class. The essay could trace Dexter's work history as a caddy and a businessman serving primarily upper-class patrons. Even at the end of the book, Dexter is a businessman who is part of the continually laboring middle class.

Robert Redford portrayed Jay Gatsby in a 1974 film version of the book.

An Overview of
The Great Gatsby

The Great Gatsby is Fitzgerald's greatest success as a novelist. It is considered a staple of the US school system's curriculum. It was first published in 1925, but the story takes place during the summer of 1922.

Nick in New York

Although *The Great Gatsby* is the story of Jay Gatsby, it is told through the eyes of his neighbor, Nick Carraway. The story begins when Nick moves from the Midwest to West Egg, a small town on New York's Long Island. He lives in a small cottage. Gatsby occupies the expansive home next to his. Upon arriving in West Egg, Nick reunites with his cousin, Daisy Buchanan, and her husband,

Tom. Their home is in the wealthy East Egg, which is more fashionable than West Egg and full of old-money families. Daisy is a beautiful, charming young woman. Tom is a loud-mouthed, thick-bodied man whose wealth allows him to ignore work and enjoy his horses and mistress. Nick also meets Jordan Baker, a female golfer. Daisy insists she will help Jordan and Nick fall in love.

Before Nick realizes what he is getting into, Tom takes him on a trip into New York City. On the way to the city, they stop off in a run-down area known as the "valley of ashes." At the local gas pump, Tom introduces Nick to the owners, George Wilson and his wife, Myrtle. When George turns his back, Tom tells Myrtle, his mistress, to meet them in the city. Nick spends the afternoon with Tom and Myrtle at their apartment, meeting Myrtle's sister and their various acquaintances. They drink throughout the afternoon and late into the evening. When Myrtle spouts off Daisy's name over and over, Tom hits her face with his strong hand, breaking her nose. Nick's memory of what happens afterward is a jumbled mess due to his own drunkenness.

Gatsby's Dream

Back in West Egg, Nick learns that his neighbor—whom he has never met—throws lavish parties in his extravagant mansion. Nick attends a party and hears several of the rumors that surround his neighbor, Jay Gatsby, and how he became so wealthy. Nick reunites with Jordan at the party and begins to like her. There is a constant flow of alcohol at the party, and every person appears to be drunk. Some of the people are singing and dancing, some are swimming and playing games, and others are arguing and crying. Jordan introduces Nick to Gatsby, who is completely sober. Gatsby's distaste for alcohol is especially ironic because many of the rumors about him say that he is a bootlegger, an illegal seller of alcohol.

One day in July, Jordan explains to Nick that before Daisy knew Tom, Gatsby and Daisy were in love and planning to be married, but Gatsby did not have enough money to support them. Instead, Daisy married Tom and his wealth. However, now that Gatsby is a wealthy man, he has moved to West Egg to reunite with Daisy. Jordan asks Nick, on behalf of Gatsby, to invite Daisy to tea at Nick's house so that Gatsby and Daisy could reunite. When Daisy sees Gatsby again, their love is quickly rekindled into an affair.

On one particularly sweltering summer day, Jordan and Nick travel with Gatsby, Daisy, and Tom into New York City to have drinks in a suite at the Plaza Hotel. On the way into the city, Tom stops at George and Myrtle's gas station while driving Gatsby's flashy yellow car. At the hotel, Gatsby and Tom begin to argue, and finally, Tom bursts out in anger that he will not let his wife have an affair, especially with such an unimportant person. Gatsby tries to explain to Tom that Daisy wants a divorce, but Tom reveals to Daisy that Gatsby earned his money through bootlegging, and her decision begins to waver. Gatsby insists that Daisy has never loved Tom, but when she appears to be torn between the two men, Gatsby's faith in her falters. Daisy insists they return home. Daisy and Gatsby leave together in Gatsby's yellow car, and Tom, Jordan, and Nick leave together shortly afterward.

The Tragedy

When Tom, Jordan, and Nick drive through the valley of ashes, they see a crowd surrounding George and Myrtle's gas station and learn that

Myrtle was killed instantly when a car hit her and did not stop. George insists that he knows the car, and Tom, Jordan, and Nick all suspect that they know the car as well. They travel home, and when Nick sees Gatsby, he guesses at the truth. Daisy was driving when Myrtle was hit. Myrtle had run out to meet the big yellow car, expecting to find Tom. To avoid hitting an oncoming vehicle, Daisy swerved and accidentally hit Myrtle. Daisy did not stop. After the tragedy, Daisy and Tom are reunited in their common selfishness, and Gatsby sees that he will never have Daisy.

The next day, Gatsby is found shot dead in his swimming pool. Tom had confessed to George that it was Gatsby's car that hit Myrtle, and George exacted his revenge on Gatsby before shooting himself. Nick arranges Gatsby's funeral, which Gatsby's father travels from Minnesota to attend. Out of the hundreds of people who flocked to his house that summer for parties, no one comes to the funeral. Nick cuts ties with Tom and Daisy, unable to face them after their reckless lives ruined the lives of others. Nick returns to the Midwest, his dreams of the East Coast's wealth and happiness dashed.

Francie Swift played Nick Carraway's love interest, Jordan Baker, in a 2000 television version of *The Great Gatsby*.

6

How to Apply Historical Criticism to *The Great Gatsby*

What Is Historical Criticism?

The goal of historical criticism is to understand the context in which a story was written. Historical criticism examines both the culture and the historical events that take place during the story and the attitudes people had toward those events. It is thus important for a historical critic to also examine the culture and history of the time when the author wrote the story. Most important, a historical critique observes how the culture and historical events impact the actions and motivations of the characters.

Here are a few questions that historical critics ask about texts: What are the major historical events surrounding the work, and how do those events affect the text? Is the text written in a distinctive historical period? How has the work been impacted by other literary or artistic works of the time period? Did any cultural trends of the time impact the author? How did the author view the cultural trends or historical events of the time period?

Applying Historical Criticism to *The Great Gatsby*

The Great Gatsby, Fitzgerald's celebrated novel, is a pamphlet for the emerging culture of the Jazz Age. Most of the characters in the novel are shining, obvious examples of Jazz Age ideals regarding love, alcohol, and leisure. The 1920s, termed both the Jazz Age and the Roaring Twenties, followed World War I and was a time of great excess in the history of the United States. Most of the characters in *The Great Gatsby* drink excessively, live lavishly while doing little work, and are sexually promiscuous. These new ideals threw out the strict propriety of the former Victorian Age and embraced the freedom of the new decade. *The Great Gatsby* is set in New York City, which a critic of the time called the new setting for American novels because of its people's lust for money, alcohol, and sex. By paying close attention to this historical context, in particular the ideals that are upheld and dashed in the book, a theme emerges. The main character, Jay Gatsby, stands apart from the others in the book because he does not fit the mold of a Jazz Age man. When Gatsby gives in to the culture of the Jazz Age, it destroys him. When he embraces Daisy and the lifestyle she leads, it marks the beginning of his tragedy.

> **Thesis Statement**
>
> The thesis statement reads: "When Gatsby gives in to the culture of the Jazz Age, it destroys him. When he embraces Daisy and the lifestyle she leads, it marks the beginning of his tragedy." If a thesis is complex, it sometimes requires two sentences to be stated clearly.

The Jazz Age was a time of public drunkenness, and the characters in *The Great Gatsby* are no exception. The novel is filled with irresponsible drinkers. In 1919, the Eighteenth Amendment to the US Constitution was ratified, outlawing the production and sale of alcohol. *The Great Gatsby* takes place during the summer of 1922, when the prohibition of alcohol was in full force. During this time in the United States, police forces were busy

> **Argument One**
>
> The author's first argument gives a historical context for the book: "The Jazz Age was a time of public drunkenness, and the characters in *The Great Gatsby* are no exception." This paragraph explains Prohibition. Without defining Prohibition, the argument would not be clear.

tracking and convicting bootleggers and smugglers who illegally distributed alcohol.

In the novel, the alcohol flows freely at the parties and homes—clearly a reflection of what was happening in US society. Tom and Daisy offer alcohol to their guests, and Tom is drinking in nearly every scene. When Tom and Nick go to Tom's apartment in the city with Myrtle, Tom gets so drunk that he violently breaks Myrtle's nose. At Gatsby's famous parties, the alcohol never runs out. When Nick meets Gatsby for the first time at one of Gatsby's parties, he is surprised that Gatsby is not drinking and imagines that it "helped to set him off from his guests."[1] Although Gatsby threw the most lavish parties in New York City during the Jazz Age, he does not fit in completely with his guests.

Although the Jazz Age promoted hard work to achieve the newly formed American dream, it also promoted frivolous spending. Because of the stock-market boom, money was easily made and freely spent. In the case of Tom and Daisy, they are

---

Argument Two

The second argument states: "Although the Jazz Age promoted hard work to achieve the newly formed American dream, it also promoted frivolous spending." This argument requires more than one paragraph to fully support it. The argument helps to set the hardworking Gatsby apart from the lounging, generationally rich Tom and Daisy.

wealthy enough through family money that Tom does not need to work. Instead, he buys horses and cars and keeps a mistress and an apartment in the city. As for Daisy, in many scenes she is described as lounging. For example, in a scene taking place on a hot summer day, Fitzgerald writes, "Daisy and Jordan lay upon an enormous couch, like silver idols, weighing down their own white dresses against the singing breeze of the fans."[2] Additionally, Daisy can hardly be bothered with raising her own daughter. Instead, the young girl spends most of her time with her nanny. Tom and Daisy are shining examples of the habits money breeds.

In some ways, Gatsby fits in with this world, but in many ways, he does not. Gatsby is the epitome of the hardworking dreamer—unlike Tom and Daisy, he must work for his money. He works because he knows that to woo Daisy, he must become rich, and this drives his every action. Although his business dealings are likely related to bootlegging, he works very hard to be successful. Gatsby is called to the phone for a business call during most of the scenes that take place at his house. His work ethic began as a young man. He even kept a book with a rigorous self-inflicted schedule of exercise, studying, sports, and work. He set goals for himself and strove to achieve them. Gatsby's father says that it was evidence that Gatsby "was bound to get ahead. He always had some resolves like this or something."[3] Although Gatsby longs for wealth, he works hard to get it, and continues working even after he has achieved financial success.

While Gatsby remains separate from the culture of the Jazz Age in regard to alcohol and work ethic, he succumbs to the Jazz Age's pursuit of sex when he begins an affair with Daisy. Tom is a man of mistresses. He openly speaks to his mistress on the phone while he has guests in his house, and without shame he takes Nick to the apartment he keeps in the city for his mistress. It is rumored that the reason Daisy and Tom left their home in Chicago was because of one of Tom's affairs. When Gatsby and Daisy reunite and begin their affair, they do it much more discreetly. Gatsby fires all of his servants so they cannot gossip about

> **Argument Three**
> The third argument is: "While Gatsby remains separate from the culture of the Jazz Age in regard to alcohol and work ethic, he succumbs to the Jazz Age's pursuit of sex when he begins an affair with Daisy." This argument shows that the change that occurs in Gatsby is brought about by Daisy.

him around town. However quiet Gatsby attempts
to keep the affair, it becomes his downfall. Gatsby
had kept himself distinct from the culture of the
Jazz Age, but once he begins his affair with Daisy,
he can no longer keep himself
separate.

Not long after the affair
begins, Gatsby's life ends in
tragedy. He is ruined by Daisy,
the woman he was willing to
do anything to have. When
Gatsby takes part in the habits
of the time, his life falls apart.
Gatsby dreams of having Daisy
as his wife, but in the end, she
chooses a safe and easy life with Tom.
When Daisy hits Myrtle with a car and does not
stop to help, it is Gatsby who pays the price.
Because of Tom, George murders Gatsby, and all of
Gatsby's dreams die with him. Daisy does not even
go to his funeral—instead, the drama of the event
draws Tom and Daisy closer and they continue
on in their carefree lifestyle. Fitzgerald writes,
"They were careless people, Tom and Daisy—they
smashed up things and creatures and then retreated

> **Argument Four**
> The fourth argument states:
> "Not long after the affair
> begins, Gatsby's life ends
> in tragedy. He is ruined by
> Daisy, the woman he was
> willing to do anything to
> have." This argument ties all
> the arguments back to the
> thesis.

Jay Gatsby's descent begins when he joins in Daisy's careless lifestyle.

back into their money or their vast carelessness, or whatever it was that kept them together, and let other people clean up the mess they had made. . . ."[4]

Conclusion
The last paragraph is the conclusion. The author summarizes all of the arguments and restates the thesis.

Jay Gatsby is a proper gentleman who sacrifices his Victorian ideals to win Daisy's love. Tom and Daisy are completely immersed in the culture of the Jazz Age. When Gatsby begins to follow the culture of the Jazz Age through his affair with Daisy, he starts toward destruction. Daisy is ultimately Gatsby's downfall, and her lack of concern for others leads to his death.

Thinking Critically about *The Great Gatsby*

Now it is your turn to assess the critique. Consider these questions:

1. The thesis asserts that Gatsby's life ends in tragedy because he takes part in Daisy's Jazz Age ideals. Do you agree that Daisy led to Gatsby's fall? Why or why not?

2. The essay says that drunkenness, spending, and sexual promiscuity were three important aspects of the culture of the Roaring Twenties. Does the narrator, Nick Carraway, take part in any of these activities? Could this information be incorporated into the essay to support the thesis?

3. The conclusion should restate the thesis and the main arguments of the essay. Does this conclusion do that effectively? Why or why not?

Other Approaches

Every type of criticism allows for multiple approaches to the text. Historical criticism can focus on the culture, historical events, or works of art from the time period of the literary work. Another historical critique of *The Great Gatsby* may focus on the stock-market boom that occurred during the writing of the novel. Another critique might focus on Fitzgerald's interpretation of the American dream within the novel.

The US Stock Market

During the 1920s, the US stock market was booming. Stock prices rose to unparalleled highs as more people borrowed money to invest in the stock market. Historical criticism analyzes how historical events influence the literature written at the time.

The thesis statement for an essay discussing the influence of the booming economy on Fitzgerald's novel could be: *The Great Gatsby* is a reflection of a society's increasing obsession with money, wealth, and social status. The tragic end to the novel is a condemnation of such a materialistic culture.

Gatsby's Dream

The American dream is one of the most important concepts in *The Great Gatsby*. Understanding how Fitzgerald defined the American dream through the novel is essential. Ronald Berman, a professor of English at the University of California, San Diego, argues that for Fitzgerald, the American dream was not about personal freedom or financial success, but about being great. Hence the title that Fitzgerald chose for his novel: *The Great Gatsby*.

A thesis statement for a related critique might be: Fitzgerald elevates Jay Gatsby above the other characters by characterizing him as hardworking and disciplined. Therefore, despite his eventual death, Gatsby does achieve the American dream.

Essential Critiques

"Bernice Bobs Her Hair" is included in a collection named *The St. Paul Stories of F. Scott Fitzgerald* that was published in 2004.

An Overview of "Bernice Bobs Her Hair"

"Bernice Bobs Her Hair" was published on May 1, 1920, in the *Saturday Evening Post* and was later included in the short story collection *Flappers and Philosophers*. "Bernice Bobs Her Hair" is often overlooked as a simple flapper story—a story about wild young women—but it offers a glimpse into a time of change in the way women were perceived.

Boring Bernice

The story likely takes place in the Midwest. Bernice, who is from Eau Claire, Wisconsin, is visiting her cousin Marjorie. Bernice is an upbeat young woman who adheres to the most proper standards, but has no social grace.

The story begins at a Saturday evening dance at a local country club, and it is apparent that Bernice is not a favorite among the young men of the area. After the dance, Bernice and Marjorie return home silently; they are not friends. Bernice has been brought up to believe that women are pursued for "mysterious womanly qualities, always mentioned but never displayed."[1] Bernice overhears Marjorie complaining to her mother that she has to take her boring cousin to all of her social events.

A Transformation

The next morning, Bernice confronts Marjorie and threatens to return home. Marjorie is willing to help Bernice leave early. Bernice is hurt further that Marjorie called her bluff and really did want her to leave. Finally, Bernice concedes that she may be able to learn how to be popular from Marjorie's instruction. Marjorie makes Bernice promise that she will follow her instructions on popularity exactly.

The key to popularity, Marjorie teaches Bernice, is to dance with the unpopular men, making them feel special. Once they feel important, they will want to dance with Bernice over and over. After a while, the most popular men will notice that the other men desire Bernice and will ask her to dance.

Becoming a Modern Woman

At the next dance, Bernice announces loudly that she is considering bobbing her hair. A bob is a short, chin-length, straight haircut. It was worn by flappers, the models of the new modern woman who thought for herself. Marjorie and Bernice have created this story to pique the interest of the men. As Bernice interacts with the young men, she follows her cousin's directions precisely, and the results are outstanding. She is soon one of the most sought-after dance partners. By the end of the evening, even Marjorie's main suitor, Warren, wants to be Bernice's partner.

The next week is a whirlwind of social engagements at which Bernice is one of the most popular young women. Although Marjorie enjoys her success at instructing Bernice, a line is crossed when Warren becomes interested in Bernice.

Marjorie becomes jealous and announces at a party that Bernice's plan to bob her hair was all an act. She would not really go through with it. The group confronts Bernice. Would she really bob her hair? When Bernice replies ambiguously that she plans to bob it, the group takes Bernice to the barbershop to get it done. Bernice winces and goes through with the haircut. She sees that the loss of her hair has made her ugly and recognizes that Warren is no longer attracted to her.

Revenge

At the dinner table, Bernice learns that the woman throwing a party in her honor believes that bobbed hair is immoral. Marjorie apologizes for encouraging Bernice to bob her hair, but Bernice sees through her words. It is the last straw for Bernice. Once alone in her room, Bernice packs her belongings to catch a late train home. But before she leaves, she takes revenge. She slips into Marjorie's room and cuts off both of Marjorie's long, beautiful braids. On her way to the train station, Bernice leaves Marjorie's braids on Warren's porch, completing her revenge.

A bob is
a women's
hairstyle that
was especially
popular in the
1920s. It was
made famous by
movie stars such
as Louise Brooks.

Essential Critiques

A 1920s flapper models the fashions of the day.

How to Apply Feminist Criticism to "Bernice Bobs Her Hair"

No. 2

What Is Feminist Criticism?

In its simplest form, feminism is the belief that women should have the same rights and respect that men have. Feminists apply this ideal to all forms of art, including literature, visual art, and music. There are two main forms of feminist criticism that began in the late 1960s. The first kind analyzes the work of male authors to determine how they depict women, while the second is the study and promotion of women's writing. These two types may overlap at times because even women's writing may contain the stereotypes, either conscious or unconscious, prevalent in the culture of the author.

When feminist criticism is applied to writing, it searches out those stereotypes to demonstrate and identify unfair portrayals of women in fiction. One such stereotype is that a woman's ultimate drive is to gain male attention and affection. Women despise other women who they deem to be competition in attaining this goal.

There are several major questions that feminists use to approach literature. How does the work represent and promote patriarchy? How does the work treat sisterhood? What female stereotypes does this work perpetuate? What does the work say about the intersection of womanhood and race, class, and other cultural factors? For works written by women, there are other questions to consider. How have the culture and critics accepted the work? How does this work fit into the canon of women's literature and how does it promote new creativity within the genre?

Applying Feminist Criticism to "Bernice Bobs Her Hair"

"Bernice Bobs Her Hair" was written in 1920 on the cusp of the Jazz Age. The Jazz Age, also known as the Roaring Twenties, created new understandings of the roles and responsibilities of men and women. Although Fitzgerald considered himself to be an advocate for the modern woman, he was not completely free of the patriarchy of his culture. In "Bernice Bobs Her Hair," two young but very different women, Bernice and Marjorie, grow close through becoming modern women. When Bernice begins to threaten Marjorie's popularity, Marjorie takes revenge and Bernice retaliates. "Bernice Bobs Her Hair" reinforces the stereotype that women will turn against sisterhood in their search for a man's attention.

At the beginning of the story, Bernice and Marjorie do not have a close relationship because they represent two different schools of thought on womanhood. Bernice is a member of the "old school" line of looking at femininity. She believes in a world where women are proper and do what they are told. Bernice's understanding of a woman comes from Victorian sensibilities. Victorian women

Thesis Statement
The last sentence of the first paragraph is the thesis statement: "'Bernice Bobs Her Hair' reinforces the stereotype that women will turn against sisterhood in their search for a man's attention." The essay is going to address two important concepts of feminist criticism: sisterhood and stereotyping.

Argument One
The first argument states: "At the beginning of the story, Bernice and Marjorie do not have a close relationship because they represent two different schools of thought on womanhood." The first argument discusses how the two main female characters in the novel demonstrate the differences between the two ideas of womanhood prevalent during the 1920s—the new, modern woman and the old, Victorian ideal.

Zelda and F. Scott Fitzgerald in the early 1920s. Zelda was a modern woman who inspired some of Fitzgerald's flapper characters.

were to be quiet and demure, relying on the thoughts of men instead of their own opinions. When Bernice quotes a text from the novel *Little Women*, Marjorie informs her that *Little Women* is out of style, a relic of their mothers' generation.

While Bernice upholds the virtues of her mother's generation, Marjorie despises them. Marjorie has discovered that she is a complex being with strong emotional and intellectual capabilities, and she cannot be the unassuming woman of her mother's generation. Marjorie asserts that girls like Bernice "are responsible for all the tiresome colorless marriages; all those ghastly inefficiencies that pass as feminine qualities."[1] Marjorie unsympathetically dashes the Victorian ideals upheld by Bernice.

During the Jazz Age, bobbed hair was the symbol of the flapper. Although Marjorie has kept her hair long, she has embodied the other ideals of the modern woman. Marjorie knows how to manipulate men for her own power. Warren is her steady date. When Marjorie asks him to do her a favor, she speaks softly and puts her hand on his shoulder. Warren readily agrees to do whatever his angel asks of him. Marjorie has learned that her intellect can produce useful results in the men around her, and she uses it to her advantage. Because Bernice has not realized the power she can hold over men, Marjorie cannot stand her.

When Marjorie teaches Bernice how to be a modern woman who attracts men, the cousins grow closer. Although Fitzgerald glorified the modern woman in most of his works, in "Bernice Bobs Her Hair," it is not until Bernice and Marjorie fit a stereotype that they become

> **Argument Two**
> The second argument states: "When Marjorie teaches Bernice how to be a modern woman who attracts men, the cousins grow closer." Here, the author addresses the feminist concept of sisterhood. The sisterhood is important for understanding the betrayal that comes later in the story.

friends. When Marjorie shares with Bernice her secret of attracting men, the two women grow closer. Marjorie attracts men by playing to their egos. She teaches Bernice to do this through the fake premise that Bernice is going to bob her hair. When Bernice asks each of the young men for an opinion on bobbed hair, she makes the men feel important.

Marjorie's goal is to feel men's admiration, and she teaches this to Bernice. Marjorie talks to her mother about "cheap popularity" and says, "It's everything when you're eighteen."[2] Although Marjorie has begun to use her intellect to get what she wants, her desires are still shaped by the patriarchal culture in which she lives. This culture tells her that her goal as a woman is to be attractive to a man.

Once Bernice is willing to listen to Marjorie's modern schemes to attract a man's attention, the two form a bond of sisterhood. Marjorie willingly coaches Bernice and congratulates Bernice when her plan works. After a dance, Marjorie does not go to speak with her mother, but instead has a nighttime discussion of the dance with Bernice. All is going well between the two girls until Warren begins to call on Bernice instead of Marjorie.

When Bernice becomes a threat to Marjorie's own ability to attract men, Marjorie exacts revenge. This blow cannot be overcome by the bonds of sisterhood they had formed. Rather than speaking with Bernice about the problem, or feeling sympathetic to the needs of her friend, Marjorie affirms stereotypical female behavior by sabotaging Bernice.

> **Argument Three**
> The third argument is: "When Bernice becomes a threat to Marjorie's own ability to attract men, Marjorie exacts revenge." This argument shows how stereotypical desires for a man's attention create a stereotypical response of revenge.

Marjorie's form of revenge demonstrates that she is not as forward thinking as she appears. When Marjorie forces Bernice to go through with bobbing her hair, both Marjorie and Bernice recognize it as pushing societal boundaries too far. Getting a bob was crossing the line. No longer was Bernice a good-girl form of the modern woman who may have been scoffed at by her mother but was accepted with her peers—she now wore the mark of a full-fledged flapper. Shuli Barzilai, an English professor at The Hebrew University of Jerusalem, explains, "Bernice wants to be an up-to-date girl, a

Argument Four

The final argument is: "Bernice confirms and reinforces this stereotype by cutting Marjorie's hair in retaliation." The author uses this argument to bring her arguments back to the beginning, addressing that despite the differences between the two main female characters' understandings of womanhood, they both resort to stereotypical behavior when their ability to attract men is threatened.

'flapper,' but belongs at heart to an older prewar order of values and behavior."[3] Marjorie knows that a man such as Warren would be attracted to an outspoken and confident woman, but he would not make a flapper his wife. By forcing Bernice to cross that line, Marjorie effectively strips Bernice of her feminine allure.

Bernice confirms and reinforces this stereotype by cutting Marjorie's hair in retaliation. Although this ending is a humorous and ironic twist, it shows the depth of the competition between the two women. When Bernice cuts her hair, it should be an act of self-expression, but it becomes her curse. Because Marjorie brought it on her, she decides to inflict the curse upon Marjorie too. The reader laughs at Bernice's act of power, but it is only an act of power over another woman. By losing her hair, which identified her as a good (and somewhat traditional) girl, Bernice loses her power over men. By cutting Marjorie's hair, Bernice makes certain that Marjorie has lost her power as well.

The story begins by demonstrating the two ideas of womanhood prevalent in the 1920s. As the two women begin to share the goal of attracting

Fitzgerald revised "Bernice Bobs Her Hair" and rewrote the last portion to give it a twist ending.

Conclusion

The last paragraph of the critique should serve as a conclusion. The conclusion summarizes the main arguments of the essay. It ends with a restatement of the thesis and concludes that Fitzgerald, as the author, chose to characterize women according to common female stereotypes.

men, their sisterhood grows despite their original differences. However, the story ends in a petty fight between the two main characters. Author Fitzgerald has reduced both women to a stereotype: women are petty and vengeful in their pursuit of men's admiration.

Thinking Critically about "Bernice Bobs Her Hair"

Now it is your turn to assess the critique. Consider these questions:

1. The thesis statement asserts that the story reinforces a stereotype about women. Do you agree or disagree? Why?

2. The arguments focus on Marjorie and Bernice's relationship. Are there other relationships or characters in the story that reinforce stereotypes about women? How could this information be used to support this thesis?

3. A conclusion should restate the thesis and main arguments. Does this conclusion leave you with more questions, or does it finish the argument of the critique well? How would you rewrite the final sentence of the critique?

Other Approaches

This critique is only one approach for applying feminist criticism to Fitzgerald's short story "Bernice Bobs Her Hair." Look back at the main questions that feminists ask. Is there another question that could be applied to this story? The following are two other possible approaches to "Bernice Bobs Her Hair." One takes the opposite viewpoint of the thesis of this critique by arguing that Bernice is empowered by cutting her hair. The other approach will demonstrate how Marjorie's mother perpetuates another female stereotype: the sweetly oblivious mother.

Empowered Bernice

In "'The Starry Heaven of Popular Girls': Fitzgerald's 'Bernice Bobs Her Hair' and Catullus's 'Coma Berenices,'" Chris M. McDonough, associate professor of classical languages at University of the South, Sewanee, in Tennessee, compares Fitzgerald's story with a classic story about a constellation. McDonough argues that Bernice is empowered by cutting her hair.

The thesis of an essay concurring with this conclusion might read: Because of similarities between the main character in Fitzgerald's short story and the classic character in the story behind the constellation known as "Coma Berenices," it is obvious that "Bernice Bobs Her Hair" is a story of women's empowerment.

One point that he makes is that in the classic story, when Berenice cuts her hair, she is rewarded by her lock of hair becoming a constellation, a sign of ascending to a powerful place. His conclusion finds that because of similarities between Fitzgerald's story and that of the constellation, it is clear that Fitzgerald wrote "Bernice Bobs Her Hair" as a story of women's empowerment through the cutting of hair.

Sweet and Oblivious Mothers

Another feminist critique might focus solely on another character in the story: Marjorie's mother. A thesis statement might read: In "Bernice Bobs Her Hair," Marjorie's mother, Mrs. Harvey, fills the stereotype of the overly sweet mother who is happily oblivious to her children's activities. One possible argument for this critique would be that when Marjorie attempts to explain to her mother the importance of "cheap popularity," Mrs. Harvey dismisses it without discussing with Marjorie the ramifications of her ideal.[4]

In the
tender
moments
of the
night
...SHOULD
LOVE
BE
ALL
THERE
IS?

For every
man and
woman who
has ever
known the
ecstasy...
and the
torment
of rapture!

JENNIFER JASON JOAN TOM
JONES · ROBARDS, JR. · FONTAINE · EWELL

20.
Century-Fox
presents

F. SCOTT FITZGERALD'S

Tender is the Night

CO-STARRING
CESARE DANOVA · JILL ST. JOHN · PAUL LUKAS
PRODUCED BY   DIRECTED BY   SCREENPLAY BY
HENRY T. WEINSTEIN · HENRY KING · IVAN MOFFAT

CINEMASCOPE
COLOR by DE LUXE

A movie poster advertises a 1962 film adaptation of Fitzgerald's
Tender Is the Night.

An Overview of
Tender Is the Night

Tender Is the Night, Fitzgerald's fourth and final completed novel, was first published serially in 1934 and then in book form that same year. It was reissued in 1951. Arriving nine years after his critically acclaimed *The Great Gatsby*, *Tender Is the Night* was seen as a disappointment by critics, especially because of its unconventional structure. The novel begins in the middle of the story. It then returns to the beginning in a lengthy flashback before returning to where the first half left off.

Book 1: Frivolous in the French Riviera

Tender Is the Night begins with a young actress named Rosemary Hoyt vacationing in the French Riviera. She finds herself among a lively group of young expatriates, including Dick and Nicole

Diver, Abe and Mary North, and Tommy Barban. Rosemary immediately falls in love with the exuberant and magnetic Dick Diver. She cannot help but love him despite his marriage to the quiet but confident Nicole.

Throughout the time that Rosemary spends with the Divers, she discovers an undercurrent of secrecy around them. A female guest at one of their parties witnesses something disturbing taking place between the Divers. She will not reveal what she has seen because Tommy, the Divers' close friend, threatens her. Despite Rosemary's uneasiness, she is overcome by her love for Dick and travels with the Divers and their friends to Paris. While in Paris, she partakes in extraordinary shopping trips with Nicole while attempting to win Dick's love.

When the group sees a man shot at the train station in Paris, Rosemary is surprised at everyone's nonchalance despite the horrific event they just witnessed. Later that evening, when Dick and Rosemary arrive back at their hotel, Rosemary finds a dead man in her bedroom. One of Dick's friends, Abe, caused the murder, although he did not kill the man himself. Dick moves the body to keep Rosemary's reputation clear. When Rosemary goes to the Divers' room to thank Dick for his help, she finds Dick comforting Nicole, who is having a mental breakdown. Rosemary now understands the secret that the Divers have been keeping: Nicole is mentally ill.

Book 2: Back to the Beginning

Book 2 begins in 1917 and chronicles the story of a fresh-faced Dr. Richard Diver as he first arrives in Europe. He is traveling to Switzerland to do research as a psychologist. At a private clinic in Zurich, he meets a beautiful schizophrenic woman named Nicole Warren. Nicole begins writing letters to Dick, and through their correspondence, her mental illness decreases dramatically. When Dick returns to the clinic, he learns from Nicole's doctor that her father sexually abused her as a child.

When Dick realizes that Nicole is in love with him, he is instructed to break off their correspondence and relationship. As he struggles to do so, he recognizes that he is also in love with her. Against the advice of the clinic's psychologists and Nicole's wealthy family, the two marry. They have two children, and Nicole's mental illness is kept in check. The story quickly passes back into the time of the first book.

After the drama in Paris, Rosemary splits from the Divers, and they set off to the Swiss Alps. There, the Divers meet up with one of the psychologists from Nicole's clinic, and he and Dick become business partners. Nicole and Dick move to the new clinic started by Dick and his business partner with the financial backing of Nicole's family money. They live peacefully for some time. During his time at the new clinic, Dick becomes increasingly restless and unhappy, relying on alcohol to dull his senses more than he will admit.

He takes a trip without Nicole and the children, where he runs into Tommy and hears that Abe was beaten to death. Dick feels that Abe's death marks the death of his own youth. The next day he receives a telegraph from New York with the news that his father has also died. Dick travels to Buffalo, New York, and attends the funeral and burial before returning to Europe. He arrives by boat in Rome and runs into Rosemary at his hotel. Rosemary is still full of love for Dick, and Dick returns her affection. They have an affair, but their passion for each other dies quickly.

Book 3: Dick's Fall Becomes Nicole's Rise

When Dick returns to his clinic, he becomes increasingly depressed and reliant upon alcohol. Dick and his business partner decide to part ways, and Nicole and Dick leave the clinic that they helped found. They return to the French Riviera, where Nicole and Dick are increasingly distant from each other. As Dick continues to drink heavily, he becomes angrier and emotionally abusive.

They run into Tommy again, and Nicole finally acts on the feelings she has for him and begins an affair. When they see Rosemary again, Dick tries desperately to regain her affection, and Nicole is disgusted by his flirtation. Tommy tells Dick that Nicole wants a divorce, and Dick resigns himself to it. Tommy and Nicole marry, while Dick returns to the United States and performs a series of unsuccessful jobs. Nicole hears from him in letters, but the letters are always from new places, suggesting that Dick never finds the happiness he desperately seeks.

The Fitzgeralds dance in front of a Christmas tree in 1925. The Fitzgeralds would face many marital problems in the following decade.

How to Apply Biographical Criticism to *Tender Is the Night*

What Is Biographical Criticism?

Authors borrow from their own experience when writing, but some stories are written from specific episodes in the author's life. Analyzing how information about the author's life relates to events that happen within a story is called biographical criticism. Biographical critics believe that the meaning of a work of art cannot be divorced from the context in which it was written. A good critique should seek to apply the author's own life experience to the works the author wrote. Studying the author's life can help illuminate the work so that it can be read in new ways. There are questions that help explain a work from a biographical standpoint. For example, what was the author saying about his or her life through this work of art?

Applying Biographical Criticism to
Tender Is the Night

Tender Is the Night was written over a period of nine years during which Fitzgerald experienced a shift in his personal happiness. The tragedy of Dick Diver in *Tender Is the Night* and Fitzgerald's own life experiences are too similar to be ignored. Fitzgerald's life events help explain the major plot events in *Tender Is the Night*. In condemning himself for the part he played in Zelda's mental illness and the eventual end of their relationship, Fitzgerald condemns his male lead character, Dick, to an unhappy life of loneliness. Instead of being driven by internal dynamics, the plot of *Tender Is the Night* is driven by Fitzgerald's self-condemnation and helplessness during a tumultuous and complex season of his own life.

The Jazz Age of the 1920s ushered in a new breed of woman. She was called a flapper or

Thesis Statement

The last sentence of the first paragraph is the thesis statement: "Instead of being driven by internal dynamics, the plot of *Tender Is the Night* is driven by Fitzgerald's self-condemnation and helplessness during a tumultuous and complex season of his own life." This essay will equate Fitzgerald's marriage with Dick and Nicole Diver's marriage and show how the plot of the novel was influenced by Fitzgerald's life.

a "new woman." <u>Fitzgerald and Dick both marry modern women</u>. Zelda Fitzgerald was a celebrity force behind shaping the US cultural idea of what this kind of woman was like. Zelda was witty and intelligent, she kept pace with the men in both smoking and drinking, and she pushed the limits of appropriate clothing and behavior whenever she could. Zelda even tried to have a career of her own, both through writing and ballet. Nicole Diver is also a modern woman, although of a quieter disposition. She is a confident woman admired for having her own ideas and intelligence apart from her husband. She also is independently wealthy of her husband and pays for her own expenses.

    <u>Zelda and Nicole are both women with mental illness, and Zelda's real-life episodes influenced the characterization of Nicole.</u> When Fitzgerald

> **Argument One**
>
> The first argument states: "Fitzgerald and Dick both marry modern women." This argument uses the historical context to understand Nicole Diver and Zelda Fitzgerald. It is also showing similarities between the lives of Fitzgerald and Dick to set up later arguments.

> **Argument Two**
>
> The second argument states: "Zelda and Nicole are both women with mental illness, and Zelda's real-life episodes influenced the characterization of Nicole." This second argument further aligns Fitzgerald's life with Dick's to show how the author's life changed the plot of the story over the period in which it was written.

began writing *Tender Is the Night*, Zelda was still mentally stable. His first drafts include no mention of mental illness. However, during the nine years he spent writing the novel, Zelda suffered a series of mental breakdowns and was diagnosed as a schizophrenic. After Fitzgerald's personal experiences with Zelda's mental illness, he began to incorporate the mental illness of Nicole into the manuscript. Nicole is also a schizophrenic, and his descriptions of her breakdowns are disturbingly accurate. In his composition notes, Fitzgerald created a table that outlined the parallels between Zelda and Nicole. From examining this table, it is obvious how closely Fitzgerald used the details of Zelda's own illness to create the story of Dick and Nicole. Zelda's mental illness and Fitzgerald's increasing sense of helplessness serve as the background for Dick and Nicole's tragic marriage. Just like Dick, Fitzgerald is ultimately unable to help cure his wife from her mental disturbance.

The major events of the Divers' marriage continue to mirror those of the Fitzgeralds'

Argument Three

The third argument states: "The major events of the Divers' marriage continue to mirror those of the Fitzgeralds' marriage through the two major affairs of the novel." This argument demonstrates how their marriages are similarly dysfunctional.

Lois Moran was a film actress who was the basis for the character of Rosemary Hoyt in *Tender Is the Night*.

marriage through the two major affairs of the novel. First, Dick has an affair with a young movie star named Rosemary Hoyt, whom he meets in the French Riviera. In reality, Fitzgerald had a crush on a young blonde actress named Lois Moran during the time he spent trying to make it big in Hollywood in 1927. Moran served as an inspiration for women throughout Fitzgerald's short stories, and ultimately for Rosemary, Dick's mistress.

Fitzgerald took a screen test and was offered a role to be the male lead in Moran's next movie, and Rosemary similarly arranges for Dick to take a screen test to be in a film with her. Although Fitzgerald's flirtation with Moran never went any deeper, it made Zelda bitterly jealous. During an argument about Moran, Zelda threw her platinum and diamond watch out the window of their train. Dick and Rosemary's affair begins as only a flirtation as well, but when it becomes more, Nicole's jealousy turns into a mental breakdown.

The second marital infidelity in *Tender Is the Night* occurs between Nicole and Tommy Barban. This affair is similar to Zelda's 1924 affair with Edouard Jozan. Tommy is a French pilot, just like Jozan was a French naval flyer. They both had experience with war that neither Dick nor Fitzgerald had known. Jozan would perform airplane tricks over the Fitzgeralds' home in the French Riviera. Fitzgerald was stunned when he learned of the affair, and it came to an end. According to biographer Andrew Turnbull, one month later, Fitzgerald wrote, "'Zelda and I close together,' and in September, 'Trouble clearing away.'" However, Turnbull wrote, "The episode was a [split] in their armor which he would never forget."[1] Nicole's affair with Tommy ends in a showdown, but it is Tommy who comes away the winner. As a result of their affair, Dick and Nicole divorce, and Nicole is remarried to Tommy.

Just like Dick and Nicole, Fitzgerald and Zelda end their lives separated. In *Tender Is the Night*, Fitzgerald's own feelings of self-doubt that contributed to the death of his own marriage influence his writing through the ultimate blaming of Dick for the collapse of the Divers' marriage. At the end of the novel, Nicole is married to Tommy and appears to be cured of her mental illness, while Dick ends up living the life of a drifter in the United States, unable to stay at a job or a town for very long. In Fitzgerald's life, he ends up separated, although never divorced, from Zelda. She continues on at mental institutions on the East Coast, while he lives in Hollywood for the rest of his short life. Dick's divorce is the final turn in his downward spiral, and he continues in his

> **Argument Four**
>
> The final argument is: "In *Tender Is the Night*, Fitzgerald's own feelings of self-doubt that contributed to the death of his own marriage influence his writing through the ultimate blaming of Dick for the collapse of the Divers' marriage." The author is showing how Fitzgerald's personal sense of helplessness shines light on the actions of Dick.

unhappiness. Meanwhile, Nicole, freed from Dick's painful descent, finally becomes a full woman, mentally sound for the first time in her adult life. The guilt that Fitzgerald harbored for the role he played in Zelda's mental illness drove this plot resolution.

Conclusion

The last paragraph of the critique serves as a conclusion. The conclusion summarizes the main arguments of the essay. It ends with a restatement of the thesis.

The depths of Fitzgerald's own personal struggles influenced the powerful story of *Tender Is the Night*. The main characters are images of real people and true circumstances from his life. Nicole is a modern woman with mental instabilities, based on the flapper image of Zelda and her struggle with schizophrenia. The affairs that lead to the end of the Divers' marriage were based on affairs that Fitzgerald and Zelda had worked through in their own marriage. The collapse of the Divers' marriage reflects the personal struggles with self-doubt that Fitzgerald felt in his marriage and in Zelda's mental breakdowns. Fitzgerald's own emotions about his complex marriage force the story to its ultimate end: the dissatisfaction of Dick.

Thinking Critically about *Tender Is the Night*

Now it is your turn to assess the critique. Consider these questions:

1. Do you agree with the thesis that because Fitzgerald relied so heavily on personal experiences for *Tender Is the Night*, the reader can assume that it betrays his own personal emotions about his life? Why or why not?

2. Biographical criticism focuses on understanding the context in which the novel was created. Do you think that context is important? Why or why not?

3. Argument one and argument two could be combined. Write a sentence that combines both of these ideas into one argument.

Other Approaches

Remember that there is not just one right critique for any story. Even within biographical criticism, there are several ways to approach *Tender Is the Night*. Another approach would be to show how Dick's early success in life and later disillusionment is similar to Fitzgerald's professional successes as a young man and the disappointments he endured later in his life. Another approach might focus on how alcoholism affected both Dick and Fitzgerald.

Early Success Holds Few Promises

A biographical approach that focuses on Fitzgerald's personal similarities to Dick would inevitably focus on their success, failure, and struggle to continue working during marriage difficulties. An effective thesis for this critique could say: While both Fitzgerald and Dick are unusually talented in their fields and experience early success, the disappointment that Fitzgerald felt later in his career as he found work difficult during his intense marriage is displayed through the failures of Dick, both in marriage and professional life. One argument would show how the longer Fitzgerald was married to Zelda and Dick was married to Nicole, the less work the men were able to accomplish.

The Other Mental Illness

Another successful biographical critique of *Tender Is the Night* could focus on how the alcoholism of Dick sprang from Fitzgerald's own struggle with it. This critique's thesis statement could read: While the most obvious mental illness in both *Tender Is the Night* and Fitzgerald's life was schizophrenia, the real relationship-altering mental illness was alcoholism. One argument for this critique might assert that both Dick and Fitzgerald refused to admit to themselves that their reliance on alcohol was affecting their abilities to work.

You Critique It

Now that you have learned about different critical theories and how to apply them to literature, are you ready to perform your own critique? You have read that this type of evaluation can help you look at literature in a new way and make you pay attention to certain issues you may not have otherwise recognized. So, why not use one of the critical theories profiled in this book to consider a fresh take on your favorite book?

First, choose a theory and the book you want to analyze. Remember that the theory is a springboard for asking questions about the work.

Next, write a specific question that relates to the theory you have selected. Then you can form your thesis, which should provide the answer to that question. Your thesis is the most important part of your critique and offers an argument about the work based on the tenets, or beliefs, of the theory you are applying. Recall that the thesis statement typically appears at the very end of the introductory paragraph of your essay. It is usually only one sentence long.

After you have written your thesis, find evidence to back it up. Good places to start are in the work itself or in journals or articles that discuss what other people have said about it. Since you are critiquing a book, you may also want to read about the author's life so you can get a sense of what factors may have affected the creative process. This can be especially useful if working within historical, biographical, or psychological criticism.

Depending on which theory you are applying, you can often find evidence in the book's language, plot, or character development. You should also explore parts of the book that seem to disprove your thesis and create an argument against them. As you do this, you might want to address what other critics have written about the book. Their quotes may help support your claim.

Before you start analyzing a work, think about the different arguments made in this book. Reflect on how evidence supporting the thesis was presented. Did you find that some of the techniques used to back up the arguments were more convincing than others? Try these methods as you prove your thesis in your own critique.

When you are finished writing your critique, read it over carefully. Is your thesis statement understandable? Do the supporting arguments flow logically, with the topic of each paragraph clearly stated? Can you add any information that would present your readers with a stronger argument in favor of your thesis? Were you able to use quotes from the book, as well as from other critics, to enhance your ideas?

Did you see the work in a new light?

Timeline

1917 Fitzgerald enlists in the US Army.

1918 Fitzgerald is stationed in Montgomery, Alabama, and meets Zelda Sayre.

1919 Fitzgerald moves to New York City to make a name for himself.

1896 Francis Scott Key Fitzgerald is born on September 24.

1930 Zelda suffers her first mental breakdown in France.

1934 *Tender Is the Night* is published serially in *Scribner's Magazine* from January through March.

Tender Is the Night is published in book format in April.

1935 *Taps at Reveille*, a collection of short stories, is published.

1940 Fitzgerald dies of a heart attack on December 21.

1920
This Side of Paradise, Fitzgerald's first novel, is published.
Flappers and Philosophers, a collection of short stories, is published.
Fitzgerald and Zelda are married on April 3.

1921
Frances Scott "Scottie" Fitzgerald is born on October 26.

1922
The Beautiful and Damned is published.
Tales of the Jazz Age, a collection of short stories, is published.

1924
The Fitzgeralds move to Europe, calling both Paris and the French Riviera home.

1925
The Great Gatsby is published.

1926
All the Sad Young Men, a collection of short stories, is published.

1948
Zelda Sayrè Fitzgerald dies on March 10.

1951
Tender Is the Night is reissued, edited by Malcolm Cowley based on Fitzgerald's notes.

1962
A film version of *Tender Is the Night* is released on February 23.

1974
A film version of *The Great Gatsby* starring Robert Redford and Mia Farrow is released on March 29.

Glossary

bourgeoisie
A Marxist term for the people who control the world's resources and maintain power over the majority of the population.

canon
A group of literary works accepted by a social group.

classism
Discrimination based upon socioeconomic class.

context
The circumstances surrounding something.

culture
The shared attitudes, values, and goals of a people or group.

elite
The superior people within a society.

expatriate
A person who has left his or her own country to live in another.

individualism
The belief that the individual is more important than the group.

Jazz Age
A term coined by F. Scott Fitzgerald to describe the historical period of the 1920s.

patriarchy
A culture in which the oldest man, usually the father, is considered the authority of the family.

patron

A person who uses the services offered by an establishment.

Prohibition

A law enforced in America from 1920 to 1933 that made the manufacturing and transportation of alcohol illegal.

proletariat

A Marxist term for the lowest socioeconomic class of a society; the working class.

promiscuous

Not restricted to one sexual partner.

serially

When a novel is published in shorter segments with a period of time between each segment, usually in a literary magazine.

socioeconomic

Relating to both the social class and the economic class of a person.

stereotype

A cultural understanding of a person based upon experiences with other people who share the same social, racial, or economic circumstances.

structure

The regular pattern for writing a plot using beginning, middle, and end.

Bibliography of Works and Criticism

Important Works

This Side of Paradise, 1920

Flappers and Philosophers, 1920

The Beautiful and Damned, 1922

Tales of the Jazz Age, 1922

The Great Gatsby, 1925

All the Sad Young Men, 1926

Tender Is the Night, 1934

Taps at Reveille, 1935

Critical Discussions

De Koster, Katie, ed. *Readings on F. Scott Fitzgerald*.
San Diego, CA: Greenhaven, 1998. Print.

De Koster, Katie, ed. *Readings on* The Great Gatsby. San
Diego, CA: Greenhaven, 1998. Print.

McNicholas, Mary Verity. "Fitzgerald's Women In
'Tender Is The Night.'" *College Literature* 4.1
(Winter 1977): 40–70. *JSTOR*. Web.

Stavola, Thomas J. *Scott Fitzgerald, Crisis in American
Identity*. New York: Barnes & Noble, 1979. Print.

Tyson, Lois. *Critical Theory Today: A User-Friendly
Guide*. New York: Garland Publishing, 1999. Print.

Winter Dreams: American Masters. PBS, 2002. Film.

Resources

Selected Bibliography

Fitzgerald, F. Scott. *The Great Gatsby*. New York: Scribner, 1925. Print.

Fitzgerald, F. Scott. *The Short Stories of F. Scott Fitzgerald*. Ed. Matthew Bruccoli. New York: Scribner, 1989. Print.

Fitzgerald, F. Scott. *Tender Is the Night*. New York: Scribner, 1934. Print.

Milford, Nancy. *Zelda*. New York: Harper Collins, 1992. Print.

Prigozy, Ruth, ed. *The Cambridge Companion to F. Scott Fitzgerald*. New York: Cambridge UP, 2002. Print.

Further Readings

Fitzgerald, F. Scott. *The Beautiful and Damned*. Mineola, NY: Dover Publications, 2002. Print.

Fitzgerald, F. Scott. *This Side of Paradise*. Amherst, NY: Prometheus Books, 2004. Print.

Turnbull, Andrew. *Scott Fitzgerald*. London, UK: Vintage, 2004. Print.

Web Links

To learn more about critiquing the works of F. Scott Fitzgerald, visit ABDO Publishing Company online at **www.abdopublishing.com**. Web sites about the works of F. Scott Fitzgerald are featured on our Book Links page. These links are routinely monitored and updated to provide the most current information available.

For More Information

The F. Scott Fitzgerald Society

www.fscottfitzgeraldsociety.org

This is a group of fans of F. Scott Fitzgerald's fiction. The group welcomes everyone, but the group focuses on an academic understanding of Fitzgerald. The Web site provides links and resources for anyone wanting to learn more about Fitzgerald. The group also has an annual international conference, a newsletter, and supports member-organized Fitzgerald activities.

The F. Scott and Zelda Fitzgerald Museum

919 Felder Avenue, Montgomery, AL 36106

334-264-4222

www.fitzgeraldmuseum.net

Visit the home where F. Scott, Zelda, and Scottie Fitzgerald lived from 1931 to 1932.

Source Notes

Chapter 1. Introduction to Critiques
None.

Chapter 2. A Closer Look at F. Scott Fitzgerald
None.

Chapter 3. An Overview of "Winter Dreams"
None.

Chapter 4. How to Apply Marxist Criticism to "Winter Dreams"

1. Lois Tyson. *Critical Theory Today: A User-Friendly Guide*. New York: Garland Publishing, 1999. Print. 50.

2. Bryant Mangum. "The Short Stories of F. Scott Fitzgerald." *The Cambridge Companion to F. Scott Fitzgerald*. Ed. Ruth Prigozy. New York: Cambridge UP, 2002. Print. 64.

3. F. Scott Fitzgerald. "Winter Dreams." *The Short Stories of F. Scott Fitzgerald*. New York: Scribner, 1989. Print. 218.

4. Ibid.

5. Ibid. 222.

6. Ibid. 234, 235.

7. Ibid. 235.

8. Ibid. 236.

9. Ibid.

Chapter 5. An Overview of *The Great Gatsby*

None.

Chapter 6. How to Apply Historical Criticism to *The Great Gatsby*

1. F. Scott Fitzgerald. *The Great Gatsby*. New York: Scribner, 1925. Print. 55.

2. Ibid. 122.

3. Ibid. 182.

4. Ibid. 187–188.

Chapter 7. An Overview of "Bernice Bobs Her Hair"

1. F. Scott Fitzgerald. "Bernice Bobs Her Hair." *The Short Stories of F. Scott Fitzgerald*. New York: Scribner, 1989. Print. 30.

Chapter 8. How to Apply Feminist Criticism to "Bernice Bobs Her Hair"

1. F. Scott Fitzgerald. "Bernice Bobs Her Hair." *The Short Stories of F. Scott Fitzgerald*. New York: Scribner, 1989. Print. 34.

2. Ibid. 30.

3. Shuli Barzilai. "'Say That I Had a Lovely Face': The Grimms' 'Rapunzel,' Tennyson's 'Lady of Shalott,' and Atwood's *Lady Oracle*." *Tulsa Studies in Women's Literature* 19.2 (Autumn 2000): 231–254. *JSTOR*. Web. 4 Jan. 2011.

Source Notes Continued

4. F. Scott Fitzgerald. "Bernice Bobs Her Hair." *The Short Stories of F. Scott Fitzgerald*. New York: Scribner, 1989. Print. 30.

Chapter 9. An Overview of *Tender Is the Night*
None.

Chapter 10. How to Apply Biographical Criticism to *Tender Is the Night*
1. Andrew Turnbull. *Scott Fitzgerald*. London, UK: Vintage, 2004. Print. 153.

Index

Index Continued

About the Author

Maggie Combs is a freelance writer and office manager. She lives in Minnesota with her husband.

Photo Credits

AP Images, cover, 3; Photofest, 12, 15, 19, 58; Jim Mone/AP Images, 20, 99 (bottom); Bigstock, 23; Library of Congress, 26; Mark Kauffman/Time & Life Pictures/Getty Images, 35, 99 (top); Paramount/Photofest, 40, 54; A&E Television/Photofest, 46; John Kobal Foundation/Getty Images, 63; Popperfoto/Getty Images, 64; Time & Life Pictures/Getty Images, 68; Hulton Archive/Getty Images, 73, 84, 89, 98; Twentieth Century Fox Film Corp./Photofest, 78